how did you feel when family... on the phone?
— Tierra Davis

I feel great knowing that I'm helping you! I feel very privileged to get to help + your story!

Dear Edith
Thank [you]
Sharing [your story]
I will never for[get] it.

...and helped us lear[n]... changed... on an unb[elievable]... — Ni[...]

...story changed... life and I wa[s]... happy when... were able to... for you. Than[k]... so much for [...] To our school... means... me and eve[ryone] else wh... ing Ger[da]

Dear Edith,
I'm so glad we [we]re a part in [re]uniting you and [G]erda! this really [w]as a life-changing [ex]perience for me.

Dear Edith, I want to let you know that your story was amazing. It really made me think about what my life would be if I had nobody, but then to find somebody that changes my life but then is also taken away. I hope that you are happy now that you will meet with your long lo[st] friend. :)
Fro[m]
M[...]

[I]'m so glad [...] [s]tuff has [hap]pened and its [cra]zy to think [...] how you [...]

Getting to actually experience what has been going on is amazing. The way I feel to have 150 eighth graders rewrite two Holocaus[t]

Mrs. Westerfe[ld]... you so... for shari[ng]... our story. It tru[ly]... as eye-opening... [s]o are so very... ou so many... people loved your... [sto]ry, and look... [fo]r...d. I'm so... [g]lad you will be... [re]united with... Gerda! It really... was the least we... [could] do for a... like you

Dear Mrs. Westerfeld,
Thank you very much for taking your time to come and see us. Your story was... touching and It is... glad that people can... the books, learn the... [Hol]oc...th about the effects of... W II. I truly hope your... union with Gerda is [soon]
Vincent Traver

Edith,
This story has impacted me deeply. I know that I will never be able to change what happened but, reuniting the two of you makes a difference. I can live my life knowing that... enhanced your life. Thank you

Dear Edith,
Thanks so much for com[ing]... you don't know how much it... to me to know that your going... actually come. I feel proud to... even met you! It's an am[azing]... Thanks so much for bringing... realization of the world [...]

# LIKE FINDING
# MY TWIN

Other books by Fern Schumer Chapman

*Is It Night or Day?*

*Motherland:*
*A Mother/Daughter Journey to Reclaim the Past*

11/8/15

To Jali —

# LIKE FINDING MY TWIN

---

## HOW AN EIGHTH-GRADE CLASS REUNITED
## TWO HOLOCAUST REFUGEES

*Fern Schumer Chapman*

## FERN SCHUMER CHAPMAN

GUSSIE ROSE PRESS

Published in 2015 by Gussie Rose Press, Lake Bluff, Illinois

Book and cover design by Tom Greensfelder

Printed by Bookmasters, Ashland, Ohio


ISBN 978-0-9964725-0-0

Library of Congress Cataloging in Publication Data

Chapman, Fern Schumer

Like Finding My Twin: How An Eighth Grade Class Reunited Two Holocaust Refugees
by Fern Schumer Chapman

1.Refugees, Jewish — Non-fiction. 2. Jews — Germany — Non-fiction. 3. Jews — United States
— Non-fiction. 4. Holocaust, Jewish (1939-1945) — Non-fiction. 5. World War, 1934-1945 —
Jews — Rescue — Fiction. 4. Child Immigrants — Unaccompanied Minors.  6. Relevancy
Project — Education — Reunion of Two Holocaust Refugees

10 9 8 7 6 5 4 3 2

To order additional copies of *Like Finding My Twin,* go online to
www.fernschumerchapman.com/store/

For Gerda Katz Frumkin

In loving memory of Zyndell Berliner Wasser (1926 – 1994)


*Give me your tired, your poor,*

*Your huddled masses yearning to breathe free,*

*The wretched refuse of your teeming shore.*

*Send these, the homeless, tempest-tost to me,*

*I lift my lamp beside the golden door.*

— Emma Lazarus, *The New Colossus*
(on the pedestal of the Statue of Liberty)


*The sincere friends of this world are as ship lights in the stormiest of nights.*

— Giotto di Bondone  (1267 - 1337)


And for my Gerdas:

Susan Figliulo, Susan Remen King, Ann Sherman,

who have guided me through crucial passages in my life.

# HISTORY

## 1933-1941

# Imagine

Imagine if you arrived home from school today and your parents said this to you:

"We know you can't understand what's happening in our country, but it's not safe for you to live here anymore. So, even though you're only 12 years old, we're sending you to a country far away where you'll live with relatives you've never met before. We hope we'll be able to come some day, and then we'll all be together again. You're leaving in two weeks, and you're going all by yourself."

Maybe your great-grandparents, grandparents, or parents came from another country to live in America. They would be called immigrants. Of course, except for Native Americans, everyone here has immigrant ancestors. But when we think of an immigrant, we don't usually think of children, much less a child traveling alone. Yet, throughout American history, many children no older than you came to this country all by themselves.

That's exactly what happened to my mother, Edith Westerfeld.

And this is her story.

*The last photograph of 12-year-old Edith with her mother and father. This picture was taken a few days before she boarded the ship to America all by herself.*

Stockstadt am Rhein

GERMANY

Scale of Miles

0        50        100

George Philip & Son, Ltd.

37

# An Interrupted Childhood

Edith's family lived in Germany, in a rural town so small, it's not even on most maps.

The town, Stockstadt am Rhein, is in the Rhein River Valley, an area famous for its delicious apples and its natural beauty. A few Jewish families were sprinkled among their Christian neighbors in each of the small towns along this part of the Rhein River.

Edith Westerfeld's family had lived in the same house in Stockstadt since the early 1700s. In 1925, when Edith was born in the family's home, there was only one other Jewish family in this town of 2000 people.

*Built by the family in 1721, the Westerfeld home was handed down from generation to generation.*

The Westerfelds were comfortable in Stockstadt for more than 200 years, and they didn't see being Jewish as being "different" from their neighbors.

In fact, the family was so completely accepted in the town that they always went to the home of a Christian neighbor to celebrate Christmas and Easter, and that family would join the Westerfelds for Jewish holidays. German first, Jewish second: That's how Edith's family thought of themselves.

*Herzliche Weihnachtsgrüsse*

*Facing page: map of Germany from 1921 with the location of Stockstadt marked by a red pin.*

*Left: contemporary German Christmas card.*

Edith's father, Siegmund, had a successful business on the first floor of their home. Siegmund helped local farmers sell their crops, and he introduced them to growing cucumbers as a cash crop. This was a big change that benefitted the farmers, and it helped establish Siegmund as a respected leader in the town.

*Edith's father, Siegmund Westerfeld.*

For his business, Siegmund installed the town's first telephone in the hallway. He didn't mind neighbors coming by to use the phone. Unfamiliar with this new technology, Edith remembers, they would yell "haaaalllloooo!" loudly into the receiver.

Siegmund often lent money to local farmers, and there weren't many families who didn't owe money to the Westerfeld business. Later, this would have terrible consequences. After all, if Siegmund went out of business, local farmers wouldn't have to pay him back. When the Nazi Party gained power, that — and much worse — happened to the Westerfeld family.

Life began to change for Edith and all of Germany's Jews in the early 1930s, when the Nazis were elected to office. Their leader, Adolf Hitler, had promised to rebuild the country, much of which was still in ruins after World War I. He also promised to restore the national pride of the German people, who had been humiliated by their crushing defeat in the war.

Once Hitler was elected, he quickly eliminated all political opposition. At the same time, he began many construction projects to restore the cities and create jobs for people who had been out of work for years. Restoring the nation's pride was another matter. The Nazis did this by appealing to prejudice.

*School photo of Edith's class taken around 1932. Seven≈year≈old Edith is sitting in the second row from the bottom, circled in red.*

The Nazis believed that Jews were "racially inferior." Many Germans shared this prejudice, but didn't act on it. A shrewd politician, Hitler used propaganda to mock "non-Germans" — especially Jews. From newspaper articles to huge popular rallies, the message went out all over Germany: Jews were responsible for the country's problems. Getting rid of Jews would purify Germany and make the nation great again.

Hitler was one of the first political leaders to communicate by radio. A master of this new technology, he provided every household with a "Nazi radio." This meant every family was able — and expected — to listen to his hate-filled speeches.

Some Germans didn't agree with Hitler's anti-Jewish crusade. But everyone could see the progress the nation was making under Hitler. People who had gone hungry for years now could provide for their families. "We saw what Hitler was doing to Jews," one German woman remembered, "but the economy was bad and we needed to make money. We looked the other way."

*Left: A Nazi radio, which Hitler distributed to every household in Germany.*

*Right: Nazi propaganda posters mocking Jews.*

Nazis were a lot like bullies on a nationwide playground — but the bullies were officially in charge. The government organized and participated in cruel behavior toward Jews, who were a minority — only one-half of one percent of the entire population. The Nazis acted in much the same way as children who exclude or bully a classmate.

As the Nazis' grip tightened, many Jews didn't understand what was happening. Siegmund couldn't believe that his neighbors and countrymen would turn against him because he was Jewish. Everyone knew he had received the Iron Cross (one of the highest honors for a German soldier) for his service in World War I. How could his neighbors, some of whom had fought alongside him, forget his bravery?

*Right: The Iron Cross, one of the highest honors presented to a German soldier.*

*Far right: Nazi party mass rally. Nuremburg, November 9, 1935.*

By 1938, when Edith was 12, it was against the law to do business or even socialize with a Jew. Customers stopped coming to Siegmund, and he had no way to make a living.

The Nazis held rallies and started organizations like the Hitler Youth, where children were encouraged to hate Jews and turn people in who didn't go along with Nazi policies. Children were obligated to report adults — even their own parents — who weren't "good Germans."

At school, Edith was the only Jew in her class. She had to sit in the corner of the room, separated from her classmates. She even had to hang her coat on a hook far from her classmates' cubbyholes. Her teacher made fun of her in class.

Above: This 1933 sign reads, "Germans, Attention! This shop is owned by Jews. Jews damage the German economy and pay their German employees starvation wages."

Left: Nazi poster which reads, "Youth serves the leader."

Near left: A textbook for German schoolchildren.

At home, Edith's friends stopped coming over to play. The owner of the local movie theater wouldn't allow her in to see the matinees on Saturday. Not one "friend" came to her birthday party. No one even answered her invitation.

Siegmund recognized that his family was in danger, and it would be best for them to leave Germany. He knew it would be difficult to get the necessary immigration papers and sponsors. He also had to convince his mother, "Oma Sarah," to leave her homeland. Siegmund wouldn't go without her. Proud of her heritage, Oma Sarah refused, saying, "I was born a German, and I will die a German."

Finally, Edith's parents had to make the most painful choice any family could face. They decided to send their daughter to another country for her own safety — even if she had to go alone. Edith's parents said that they would soon come to America, so she didn't need many pictures of her family. She only packed two small passport photos of her parents, and a few pictures of herself with them.

One thing Edith insisted on taking was her favorite doll, which her mother had made for her eighth birthday. But there wasn't any room in her suitcase for "Arno," so Edith carried him in her arms as she left her home for the last time.

*Left: a doll from the 1930s. Above Right: Oma Sarah.*

*Below Right: Passport photos of Edith's parents that they hurriedly placed in the bottom of her suitcase. Frieda and Siegmund Westerfeld had hoped to follow Edith to America. For years, these were the only pictures Edith had of her parents.*

# The Voyage Begins

*Children flee Germany to travel abroad without their parents.*

With 10 other children, ranging in age from four to 16, Edith boarded the cruise ship "Deutschland" on a cold gray day in March 1938. (Flying across the Atlantic Ocean was far too risky for passengers in those days.) Each child wore a tag with an assigned number around his or her neck. That number served as a kind of mailing address, telling who the child was and where he or she was going. Edith was headed for Chicago, a place as foreign as the moon, to live with an aunt and uncle she had never met.

During the 10-day trip, a young German woman chaperoned the children on the "Deutschland." But Edith remembers that the chaperone was more interested in the ship's parties than doing her job, so the children were mostly left alone.

Within hours of setting sail for America, the children began making friends. Edith met another 12-year-old girl, Gerda Katz. They spent all their time together on the ship, eating, playing, and even taking care of one another.

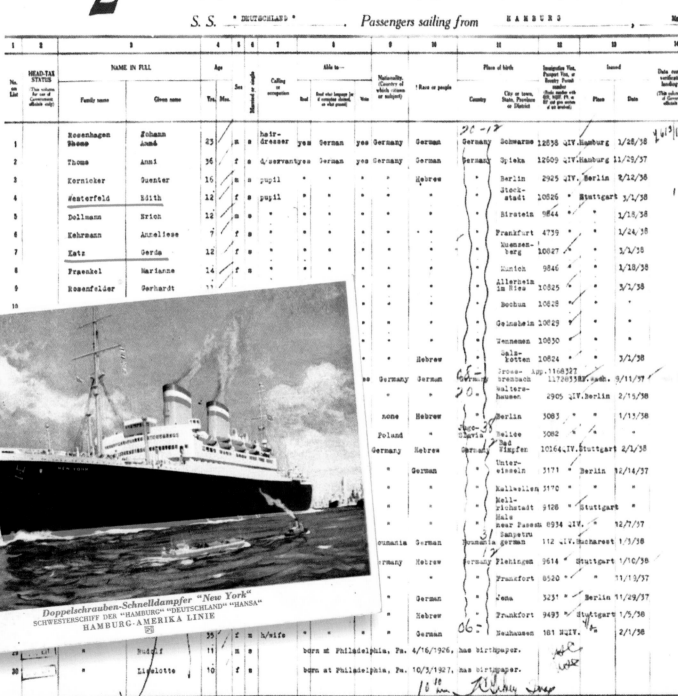

*Right: The list or manifest of "Alien Passengers for the United States" for March 10, 1938. Edith Westerfeld and Gerda Katz are listed as passengers, numbers 4 and 7, on this U.S. document.*

*Below: A postcard of the "SS New York," the sister ship of the "SS Deutschland" that brought Edith to America in 1938.*

Many passengers became seasick during the voyage as the "Deutschland" sailed through violent storms. Gerda was so sick, she couldn't raise her head from her pillow. Edith sat with her as the ship plunged through huge waves, its lights flickering. Both girls were terrified, but at least they had each other.

One evening, when the seas were calmer and Gerda felt better, she showed Edith the special gift her mother had packed for her: an old-fashioned framed picture with a German poem called "Mutter" (Mother).

### Mother

Whether at home or in a foreign land,
You are never alone.

Your mother's love follows you,
accompanying you wherever you go.

She is with you on your way;
She thinks of you all of her days.

No matter how much work she has,
She thinks of you when you have worries.

When you are looking for rest and solace,
She tells you, don't hurry today, don't make
yourself problems.

She stands behind you when you are alone:
In these moments, you see how lost you are
without your mother.

Gerda and Edith began to feel like twins — so close, they could experience one another's pain. They were not biological sisters, but their parents had made the same wrenching decision to send their young daughters, all by themselves, to safety in America. In their hearts, Gerda and Edith shared the same deep, uprooting loss.

# Historical Twins

As she said good-bye to her daughter at the port, Gerda's mother gave Gerda this gift – a newspaper clipping of a poem that describes a mother's role in her child's life.

1938 passport photos for Gerda Katz (above) and Edith Westerfeld (below).

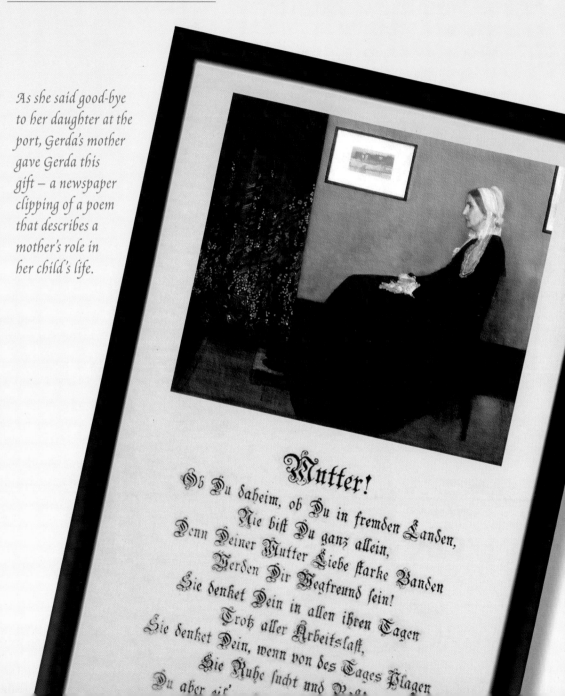

## Mutter!

Ob Du daheim, ob Du in fremden Landen,
Nie bist Du ganz allein,
Denn Deiner Mutter Liebe starke Banden
Werden Dir Wegfreund sein!
Sie denket Dein in allen ihren Tagen
Trotz aller Arbeitslast,
Sie denket Dein, wenn von des Tages Plagen
Sie Ruhe sucht und R...
Du aber si...

At the same time, though, they also shared a scary and exciting adventure. Together, Edith and Gerda got their first taste of independence, with no one to tell them what to do or when to do it. At its best, life on the ship was a banquet of fun and food.

Back in Germany, fresh fruit, vegetables and luxuries like chocolate were rare and expensive during the Great Depression and, later, World War II. But on board the "Deutschland," the children could eat as much fruit, dessert, and chocolates as they wanted. Of course, there was no school, so they were allowed to stay up as late as they wanted to.

At the end of the 10-day journey, the children were ready to leave

*Left: brochure and menu from the "SS Deutschland."*
*Above: dessert buffet from a cruise ship in the 1930s.*

101A—

POST CARD

THIS SPACE FOR ADDRESS ONLY

PLACE STAMP HERE

MADISON 1938

Mr. Lautenschläger

Stockstadt a/Rh

Hintergasse

Germany.

*Left: Just after arriving in New York, Edith wrote a family friend this postcard: "My dear Mina, Yesterday we arrived in NY and I send my lovely parents greetings and kisses. Your Edith Westerfeld."*

*Below: In parting, Gerda gave Edith one of her passport pictures. She wrote on the back: "In Remembrance. Your friend, Gerda Katz." For 72 years, Edith kept this photo in a safe place; it was the only remnant of Edith and Gerda's friendship.*

the sea-sickening ship. After landing at Ellis Island, the young refugees found themselves in a new world of skyscrapers, elegant shops, water fountains, elevators, and strange foods like breakfast cereals and soda pop.

A Jewish organization treated the children to a few dreamlike days in New York City. They shopped on Fifth Avenue, went to the top of the Chrysler Building, and even saw the brand-new Disney movie, "Snow White and the Seven Dwarfs" at Radio City Music Hall.

All the children were reluctant to leave their "family" of ship friends, but their New York holiday had to end. Edith and Gerda boarded trains to meet their new families — Edith in Chicago, Gerda in Seattle. The girls parted tearfully on March 21, 1938. Edith gave Gerda her address, and Gerda promised to write her. Gerda gave Edith her passport picture and wrote a special message on the back of it.

And then, they were gone — as lost to one another as their families back in Germany.

After 10 days on the "Deutschland," three days touring New York City, and 15 1/2 hours on the train, Edith arrived in Chicago. There, she would live with Uncle Jack and Aunt Mildred, whom she had never met before. Uncle Jack had gone to Chicago long before Hitler came to power.

Like many families during the Great Depression, Uncle Jack and Aunt Mildred had a hard time just paying their rent. They were glad to give Edith a place to live because, like all "host families," they were paid $48 each month by the Jewish organization that had brought the children to America.

*Aunt Mildred and Uncle Jack. Jack, Siegmund's brother, left Germany and came to the USA around 1915. He married Mildred, an American.*

But many families treated the children more or less like servants. Aunt Mildred expected Edith to do all the laundry, scrub the toilets, clean the kitchen, take out the garbage, and wax the floors. In the small two-bedroom apartment, Edith slept on a couch in the living room and kept her belongings in the linen closet. Many nights she stayed up late, waiting for everyone to go to bed so she could finally go to bed, too.

Fitting in at O'Keefe Elementary School was just as difficult for Edith as adjusting to life with Aunt Mildred

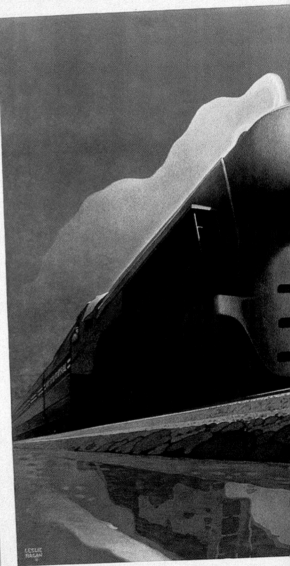

THE *New* 20TH CENTUR

NEW YORK—*16 hour*

and Uncle Jack. On her first day of school, the principal placed Edith in a first-grade class because she didn't speak English. As her language skills improved, she moved up from one grade to the next, but at every level, her classmates teased her.

Once the United States entered WWII and Germany was the enemy, Edith endured even more bullying. Her classmates called her cruel names like "kike" and "kraut." She didn't know quite what the words meant, but she knew that, just as she had been the outsider as a Jew in Germany, she was the outsider as a Jew and a German in America. Even now, 75 years after those difficult days, Edith still remembers a classmate named Doug. Why? "Because, unlike the other students," she says, "he smiled at me and made me feel welcome."

O'Keefe Elementary School, Chicago

*Above: Elementary school classroom from the 1930s.*

*Center Left: "The 20th Century Limited." Edith took this new train from New York to Chicago, making the trip in a record-breaking 15 1/2 hours.*

*Center Right: One of the anti-Semitic headlines in Henry Ford's weekly, "The Dearborn Independent," May 22, 1920. All Ford dealers were required to sell the paper.*

The Ford International Weekly

# THE DEARBORN INDEPENDENT

Dollar  Dearborn, Michigan, May 22, 1920  Five Cents

## The International Jew: The World's Problem

LIMITED

CHICAGO

Edith often wondered how Gerda was doing in Seattle. If only she and Gerda could have stayed together, Edith believed, then everything would be better. If only Gerda would write, Edith kept thinking, then she wouldn't feel so alone.

Making matters worse, Edith heard almost nothing from her parents because the German government stopped many of their letters. She worried about her parents constantly, and she didn't understand why she couldn't have stayed in Germany with her family. At times, she thought, "Did they send me away because they didn't love me?"

A German friend from home sent the photograph on the right to Edith almost sixty years later. The photo shows Edith's mother with a girl about Edith's age. A neighbor said that Frieda missed Edith terribly and had come to love this young girl, trying to fill the emptiness in her heart. Just a year after this picture was taken, Edith's parents and grandmother were taken to concentration camps and murdered.

# RESEARCH
## APRIL 2011

# Sharing Edith's Story

Many years later, after Edith grew up, became a nurse, and had two children, I shared her story with the eighth-grade class at Madison Junior High School (MJHS) in Naperville, Illinois. It was spring, 2011, and the students had just read my book, *Is It Night or Day?* After I finished my talk, one student asked, "But what happened to Gerda?"

It was a question I couldn't answer.

"Haven't you tried to find Gerda?" she persisted.

"Yes, sure, I've looked online," I said. "But she may have married and changed her name, so I don't even know who I'm looking for." I thought about Gerda's tiny passport photo — all that remained of Edith and Gerda's friendship — a dim, unhelpful picture of a girl with curly brown hair and a spray of freckles.

My mother had been asking me the very same question for years. After reading an early version of *Is It Night or Day?*, she said, "I hope this book is an invitation for Gerda to find me. That's my greatest wish: to see Gerda again."

"Why is Gerda so important to you?" I asked.

"She is the closest I will ever get to family," she said.

**Far right: Fern presents the story of Edith to a junior high school class.**

**Near right: the cover of *Is It Night or Day?***

Fern Schumer Chapman

www.fernschumerchapman.c

Email: fernschumer@aim.com

# Why Can't We Find Gerda?

As children of the social-networking age, the MJHS students couldn't imagine how anyone could remain out of touch with anyone else, anywhere in the world. "After we heard that the two girls never met up, it really hurt," said 14-year-old MacKenzie Sisko. "We couldn't imagine not ever seeing your best friend again."

When the students returned to their classrooms, Jessica Deutsch approached her social studies teacher, Catie O'Boyle. "Can't we do something?" Jessica asked. "Why can't *we* find Gerda?"

Spotting an opportunity, Mrs. O'Boyle agreed to let the students spend a couple of weeks' class time on Gerda's trail.

The students' early research turned up a little-known program called "The 1,000 Children Project." Organized by Quaker, Lutheran, and Jewish groups, the project brought children ranging in age from 14 months to 16 years from Nazi Germany to America. To avoid opposition from anti-Jewish forces in the United States, the organization operated quietly, sending just a few children at a time on cruise ships. Between 1934 and 1945, the program saved about 100 children a year, ultimately rescuing some 1,400 children.

**Mrs. O'Boyle (left) agreed to let the MJHS students spend a couple of weeks' class time on Gerda's trail.**

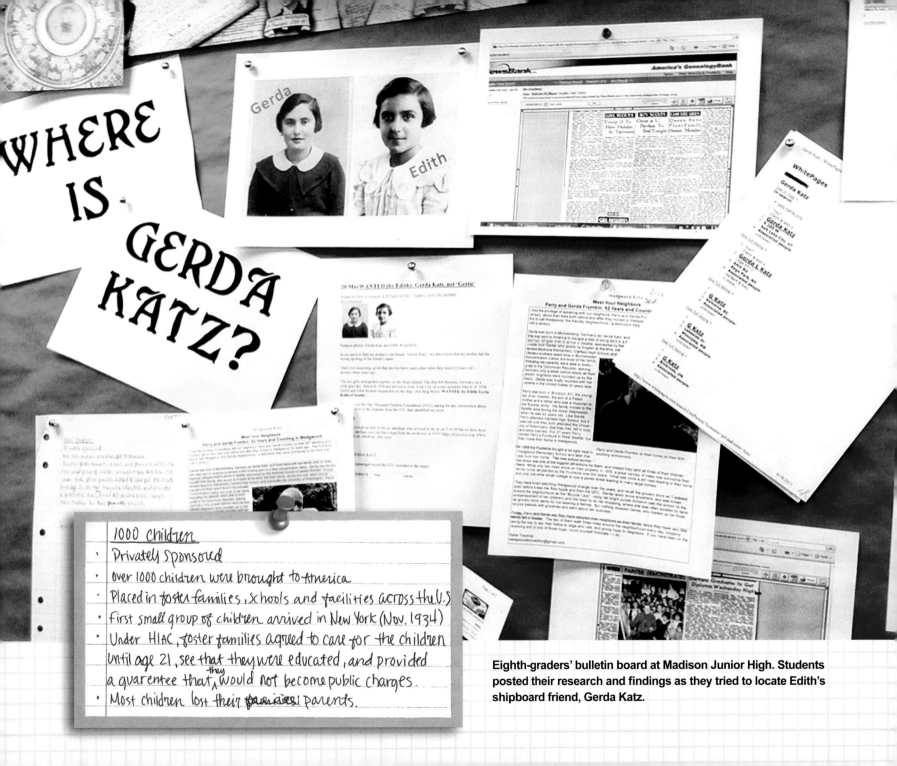

WHERE IS GERDA KATZ?

**1000 children**

- Privately Sponsored
- Over 1000 children were brought to America
- Placed in foster families, schools and facilities across the U.S
- First small group of children arrived in New York (Nov. 1934)
- Under HIAC, foster families agreed to care for the children until age 21, see that they were educated, and provided a guarantee that they would not become public charges.
- Most children lost their ~~families~~ parents.

**Eighth-graders' bulletin board at Madison Junior High. Students posted their research and findings as they tried to locate Edith's shipboard friend, Gerda Katz.**

# Finding Gerda Katz

With only Gerda's name, the name of the ship, and Gerda's destination of Seattle, Mrs. O'Boyle's eighth graders scoured thousands of online sources that might give them information. They tried different spellings of Gerda's name. They looked in different locations. Within a day they had come up with four people named Gerda Katz: One in New York, two in Canada, and one without an address.

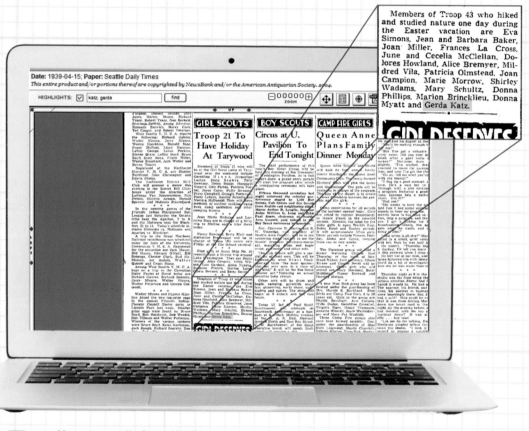

**1** Newspaper clip from 4/15/39, *Seattle Daily Times*: Gerda Katz is listed as a member of Girl Scouts Troop 21.

**2** Newspaper clip from 6/10/1945, *Seattle Daily Times*: Gerda Katz is listed as a graduate of Garfield High School.

Then they found someone in Seattle. A *Seattle Daily Times* newspaper clipping dated April 15, 1939, listed a Gerda Katz as a member of Girl Scout Troop 43. They soon found another article in the *Times* on June 10, 1945, listing the graduating class of Garfield High School — including a Gerda Katz.

The real breakthrough came a few days later, when students reading wedding announcements in the *Seattle Daily Times* learned that a Gerda Katz had been married on July 16, 1950. Now the students knew they were looking for Gerda Katz Frumkin and they could search for more recent references.

**3** Newspaper clip from 12/28/1949, *Seattle Daily Times*: Gerda Katz is engaged to marry Joseph Perry Frumkin.

A crucial piece of information came from a small community online newsletter, *The Wedgwood Echo*, in which the students found a 2010 article marking the 60th wedding anniversary of Perry and Gerda Frumkin. Gerda, the article mentioned, was born in Munzenberg, Germany, and "was sent to America to escape a fate of being sent to Nazi concentration camp." The newspaper clipping convinced students that they had found the "right" Gerda Katz.

**4** Newspaper clip from 7/16/1950, *Seattle Daily Times*: Gerda Katz marries Joseph Perry Frumkin.

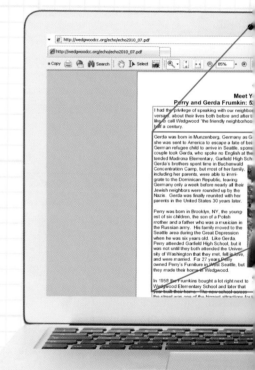

**5** In a *Wedgwood Echo* article announcing the 60th anniversary of Gerda and Perry, students learned that this was the Gerda Katz they were looking for.

As Mrs. O'Boyle read the article out loud, the students gasped. "That's it!" one shrieked, high-fiving the girl next to her. Other students whooped; some got up and danced. "We found her!"

...a was born in Munzenberg, Germany as Gerda Katz, and lived there with her family until, in 1938, ...was sent to America to escape a fate of being sent to a Nazi concentration camp. Gerda was the first ...han refugee child to arrive in Seattle, sponsored by the National Council of Jewish Women. A local ...le took Gerda, who spoke no English at the time, into their family, where she was raised and at-...ed Madrona Elementary, Garfield High School, and eventually the University of Washington. Two of ...la's brothers spent time in Buchenwald ...centration Camp, but most of her family, ...ding her parents, were able to immi-...e to the Dominican Republic, leaving ...many only a week before nearly all their ...sh neighbors were rounded up by the ...s. Gerda was finally reunited with her ...nts in the United States 30 years later.

...r was born in Brooklyn, NY, the young-...f six children, the son of a Polish ...er and a father who was a musician in ...tussian army. His family moved to the ...tle area during the Great Depression ...e he was six years old. Like Gerda, ...y attended Garfield High School, but it ...not until they both attended the Univer-...f Washington that they met, fell in love, ...were married. For 27 years Perry ...ed Perry's Furniture in West Seattle, but ...made their home in Wedgwood.

*Perry and Gerta Frumkin at their home on their 60th wedding anniversary.*

...58 the Frumkins bought a lot right next to ...gwood Elementary School and later that

# First Emails

Mrs. O'Boyle found an email address for a Gerda Katz Frumkin online. To confirm that the class had found the right Gerda Katz, Mrs. O'Boyle sent this message on April 23, 2011:

> Mrs. Frumkin,
>
> I am really hoping that you are the Gerda Katz we are looking for. We had an author visit our school recently and she told us your story and the story of your friendship with Edith Westerfeld on the *Deutschland* in March of 1938. I have 150 students who are very anxious to hear if you are "our Gerda Katz," as we have come to know her.
>
> Catie O'Boyle
> Social Studies teacher
> Madison Jr. High School

A week later, when I was out of town, I received an urgent-sounding voicemail from my mother. "Call me as soon as you can," she said. That was all.

I called her back. When she heard my voice, she fell silent.

Edith (left) hears from Gerda for the first time in 70 years. Gerda had learned about Edith after receiving an email from Mrs. O'Boyle (below).

"Mom, what's happened?" My heart was pounding. Gasping and clearing her throat, she tried to find words.

"What is it, Mom?" She was 86 years old, and I worried about her. Finally, she managed one word, her voice brimming with the excitement and emotion of a 12-year-old:
"G – G – Gerda."

"What about her?"

"She... she... wrote me."

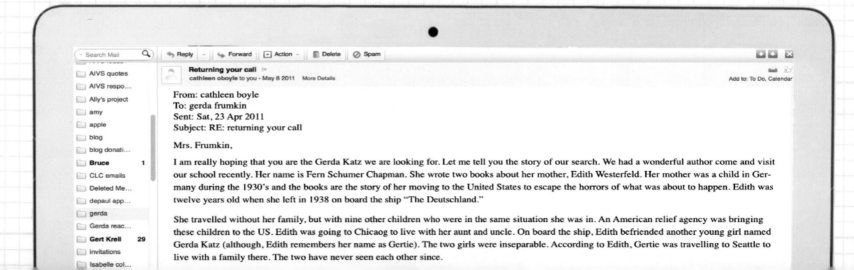

Returning your call
cathleen oboyle to you - May 8 2011    More Details

From: cathleen boyle
To: gerda frumkin
Sent: Sat, 23 Apr 2011
Subject: RE: returning your call

Mrs. Frumkin,

I am really hoping that you are the Gerda Katz we are looking for. Let me tell you the story of our search. We had a wonderful author come and visit our school recently. Her name is Fern Schumer Chapman. She wrote two books about her mother, Edith Westerfeld. Her mother was a child in Germany during the 1930's and the books are the story of her moving to the United States to escape the horrors of what was about to happen. Edith was twelve years old when she left in 1938 on board the ship "The Deutschland."

She travelled without her family, but with nine other children who were in the same situation she was in. An American relief agency was bringing these children to the US. Edith was going to Chicaog to live with her aunt and uncle. On board the ship, Edith befriended another young girl named Gerda Katz (although, Edith remembers her name as Gertie). The two girls were inseparable. According to Edith, Gertie was travelling to Seattle to live with a family there. The two have never seen each other since.

She then forwarded to me the email she had received earlier in the day.

Dear Edith,

I have thought of you often and am so thankful that you found me. Can't wait until we speak together…

With love,
Gerda

---

Mrs. O'Boyle's eighth graders had hoped that Gerda and Edith would reunite at Madison Junior High, but Gerda had been ill and wasn't able to travel. Instead, the school invited my mother and me for a day of celebration.

Stepping through the school's front doors on a bright, unusually warm day in May, we stopped before a large glass display case bursting with yellow origami boats – 1,000 of them, to be exact.

"We folded each of them to represent each of the 1,000 children that America saved," Jessica Deutsch told us. "It took, like, forever. They're all yellow, except the ones that represent the other refugee children on the ship that brought Edith to America.

Gerda (left) contacted Edith by email. MJHS students' art project (below) of 1,000 yellow origami boats, including eight red boats symbolizing the other children and two green boats for Edith and Gerda.

The two green ones represent Edith and Gerda and their special friendship."

As my mother and I entered the large media center, the school band played a song they had learned for the occasion: "My Country, 'Tis of Thee." The trombone player's puffy cheeks were red with effort and moist with tears.

Making our way through the room, we squinted up at a screen displaying an image of an elderly woman with short, red hair and a bald-headed man, sandwiching in their embrace a beaming teenager with long, wavy brown hair.

"Who's that?" my mother turned to ask me. I had the answer because Ms. O'Boyle had sent me a copy of the photo earlier that day.

"It's Gerda, her husband, and their granddaughter," I told her.

"Oh, my God!" she gasped. The image looked nothing like the picture of 12-year-old Gerda that Edith had kept in her mind and heart for nearly eight decades. She was just beginning to see how these eighth graders had changed her world.

**2011 photo of 86-year-old Gerda Katz; her 19-year-old granddaughter, Rebecca Sherman; and her husband, Perry Frumkin. Mrs. O'Boyle projected this photo on a screen as Edith entered the school's Media Center to meet with students.**

# REUNION
## JULY 2011

# Like Finding My Twin

Just a few weeks later, in July, our family flew to Seattle to meet Gerda and her family. Producers at the Oprah Winfrey Network (OWN) had heard about the Madison Junior High students, and they helped arrange the reunion of the two women.

Before the dramatic moment of reunion, the crew interviewed Gerda and Edith separately to explore how each felt about seeing the other again. Because I had written two books telling my mother's story, Edith was well-prepared to face her past. "I can't wait," my mother said. "This is a dream come true. It's almost like finding my parents again."

Gerda, on the other hand, had buried her painful past so deeply, not a single person in her life knew about her tragic family history. Even Gerda's daughter, Ann Sherman, knew almost nothing about her mother's German childhood and immigration.

"Do you remember a girl on the ship named Edith?" Ann asked Gerda after Mrs. O'Boyle's email arrived. "No!" Gerda said.

But when Ann showed her Edith's old passport picture, Gerda burst into tears. "My Edith!" Memories flooded her; she cried for the next two weeks.

The two old friends would speak—more or less—just once before meeting face-to-face. On the phone, each said hello and then they sobbed together for the next 20 minutes, gasping and moaning, barely uttering a word.

Above: Gerda with her daughter, Ann.

Below: Fern arrives in Seattle.

# The Reunion!

Edgy and fidgety just before the reunion, my mother, my 20-year-old daughter, and I waited in a hotel room at the grand Fairmont Olympic Hotel in downtown Seattle, as the TV production crew organized the meeting.

Finally, the OWN producers called us, and my daughter and I escorted Edith into the ballroom. There was Gerda, seated on a sofa, next to her daughter, Ann, and Ann's daughter, Rebecca.

When Gerda spotted Edith, she jumped right off the sofa. Both her arms shot straight up in joyful thanks.

"Why didn't you write?" Edith asked as they hugged. For decades, Edith had wondered why Gerda never got in touch after the girls parted.

Gerda was startled. "I lost your address," she explained.

Edith had interpreted Gerda's silence as another painful abandonment. But with these few words, Edith was ready to pick up where she and Gerda had left off. For the next few days, the two women held hands whenever they were together.

They sprinkled their conversations with the German they remembered, falling easily back into the enduring friendship they had established on the *Deutschland* in 1938.

Gerda and Edith meet with the students who reunited them and changed their lives.

# Reflections

For Mrs. O'Boyle's eighth graders, the experience of reuniting Gerda and Edith offered students an opportunity to reflect on their own values.

 "We all know that feeling we have when we first read about the horrors -- whether it's what happened to Native Americans, slaves, or Holocaust victims," Mrs. O'Boyle told the assembled audience on the day Gerda and Edith visited Madison Junior High and met with the students who reunited them. "We feel totally and completely inadequate. We can do nothing," she said, her voice cracking. "It makes us think we would be better. We wouldn't do what they did. But we never have the chance to go back in history and stop it, or be that better person.

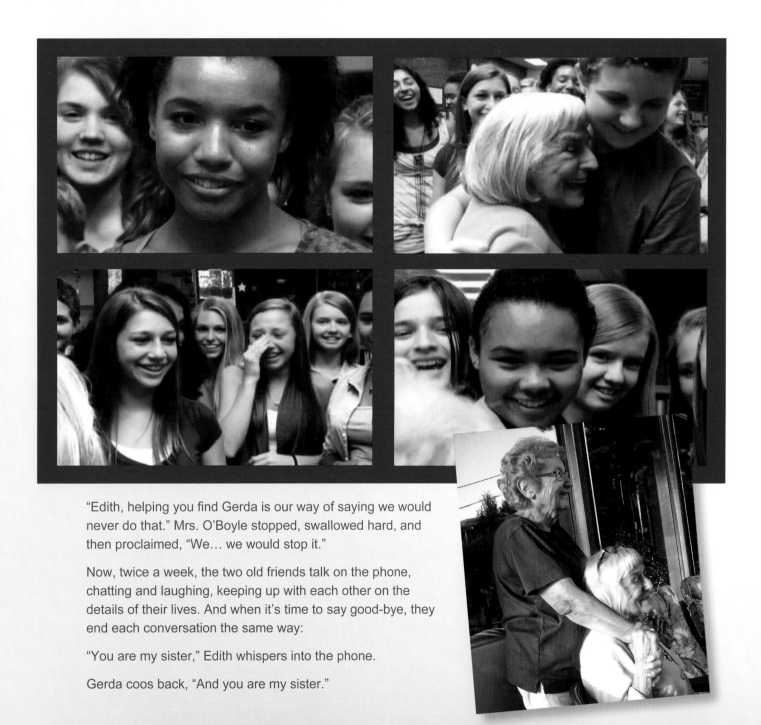

"Edith, helping you find Gerda is our way of saying we would never do that." Mrs. O'Boyle stopped, swallowed hard, and then proclaimed, "We... we would stop it."

Now, twice a week, the two old friends talk on the phone, chatting and laughing, keeping up with each other on the details of their lives. And when it's time to say good-bye, they end each conversation the same way:

"You are my sister," Edith whispers into the phone.

Gerda coos back, "And you are my sister."

Some of the 1,000 children get their first look at the Statue of Liberty as their ship approaches the New York Harbor in 1938.

# COMING TO AMERICA AS CHILDREN

Throughout our nation's history, children have come to this country by themselves for all sorts of reasons — war, famine, political persecution, economic hardship, natural disasters. For example:

- During the Irish Potato Famine of the late 1840s, parents who couldn't afford to feed their children would send them on ships to America. The sad scenes at the docks were called "American wakes."

- British families sent their children to safety in America during the German blitz of England during World War II.

- Cubans sent their children to Miami for safety during *Operation Pedro Pan* in the 1960s.

- More than 27,000 child refugees have fled the Sudanese Civil War to come to America.

- Parents in Mexico and Central and South America, who desperately want their children to have a better education and a safer life in the United States, send their sons and daughters to live with relatives in this country. Nearly 68,000 "unaccompanied minors" crossed the border to the United States illegally in 2014, They are known as "undocumented residents" and face many legal obstacles to education and opportunities throughout their lives.

Whatever the reason for leaving their countries, many child immigrants have separated painfully from their families and their homes. Some experience a cold absence of love in their new environment. One of the "One Thousand Children" said that after he left Germany, no one ever hugged him again throughout his childhood. These dramatic uprootings often cast these young people adrift, even as they are rescued.

# PHOTO CREDITS

Cover photo of children fleeing - http://www.ushmm.org/wlc/en/article.php?ModuleId=10005139

Endpages, notes from Madison Junior High School students - Courtesy of Catie O'Boyle, Social Studies teacher at Madison Junior High School

Photo of Edith, Frieda, and Siegmund Westerfeld - Edith Westerfeld Schumer's personal collection

German map - http://www.philatelicdatabase.com/maps/germany-map-1921/

Photo of Stockstadt - http://de.academic.ru/dic.nsf/dewiki/1335074

Christmas card - http://www.clipartandcrafts.com/vintage-graphics/christmas/index.htm

Photo of house - Edith Westerfeld Schumer's personal collection

Poster of cucumbers - http://catalogue.swanngalleries.com/

Photo of Siegmund Westerfeld - Edith Westerfeld Schumer's personal collection

Class photo - Edith Westerfeld Schumer's personal collection

Cover of *Mein Kampf* - http://www.ushmm.org/learn/introduction-to-the-holocaust

Image of Nazi radio - http://tomahawkfilms.com/blog/?p=2169

Nazi propaganda - http://www.ushmm.org/learn/holocaust-encyclopedia, http://www.holocaustresearchproject.org/holoprelude/index.html, http://www.slideshare.net/Pentucket/ashley-cook-8-stages-of-genocide, http://www.chgs.umn.edu/histories/otherness/otherness1-2.html, http://www.chdhu.org/collections.asp

Nazi march - https://commons.wikimedia.org/wiki/File:Reichsparteitag_1935.jpg

Iron Cross - https://en.wikipedia.org/?title=Iron_Cross

Nazi poster, "Youth serves the Leader" - http://sitemaker.umich.edu/youthunderfascism/home

German textbook - http://designobserver.com/feature/branding-youth-in-the-totalitarian-state/6957/

Photo of 1933 Nazi boycott - http://en.wikipedia.org/wiki/Nazi_boycott_of_Jewish_businesses#/media/File:Boycot_of_Jewish_shops_april_1_1933.jpeg

1930s doll - http://themadhattedbear.blogspot.com/2011_03_01_archive.html

Photos of Oma Sarah, passport pictures of Frieda and Siegmund Westerfeld - Edith Westerfeld Schumer's personal collection

Children fleeing Germany - http://www.ushmm.org/wlc/en/article.php?ModuleId=10005139

Postcard of *New York* ship - Jürgen Flügge collection, http://www.hof-theater-tromm.de

Ship manifest - Hebrew Immigrant Aid Society, http://www.hias.org/

Passport picture of Gerda Katz - Gerda Katz Frumkin personal collection

Passport picture of Edith Westerfeld Schumer - Edith Westerfeld Schumer personal collection

Newpaper clipping of the poem, "Mutter" - Gerda Katz Frumkin personal collection

*Deutschland* Brochure and Menu - http://www.gjenvick.com/SteamshipLines/HamburgAmericanLine/index.html

Photo of buffet on cruise ship - http://cruiselinehistory.com/september-8-2009-marks-the-75th-anniversary-of-the-luxury-liner-morro-castle-disaster/

Postcard of New York City World's Fair 1939 - Jürgen Flügge collection, http://www.hof-theater-tromm.de

Back of Gerda's passport picture - Edith Westerfeld Schumer personal collection

Picture of Aunt Mildred and Uncle Jack - Edith Westerfeld Schumer personal collection

*20th Century Limited* poster - http://www.american-rails.com/20th-century-limited.html

*Dearborn Independent* clip - http://www.hist-chron.com/USA/EncJud_juden-in-USA05_1920-1929.html

1938 class - http://www.digitalhorizonsonline.org/cdm/ref/collection/uw-ndshs/id/3774

O'Keefe Elementary School - https://chicagohistoricschools.wordpress.com/2014/01/12/isabelle-okeeffe-elementary-school/

Photo of Frieda and girl - Edith Westerfeld Schumer personal collection

Photo of Fern Schumer Chapman speaking - Photo by Diane Buerger, Art Teacher at Orland Junior High School

Photo of Mrs. O'Boyle and students - screen captures from the OWN show

Bulletin board from students' research - Fern Schumer Chapman personal collection

Photos of Edith and Gerda - screen captures from the OWN show

First email - Catie O'Boyle collection

Second email - Edith Westerfeld Schumer personal collection

Photo of yellow origami boats - Courtesy of *The Daily Herald*

Photo of Gerda; her husband, Perry; and granddaughter, Becca Sherman - Gerda Katz Frumkin personal collection

Photo of Gerda and daughter, Ann Sherman - screen capture from the OWN show

Photo of Fern arriving in Seattle - Larry Breitkopf

Pictures capturing the reunion - screen captures from the OWN show

Last picture of Edith and Gerda - Larry Breitkopf

Picture of the 1,000 children approaching the Statue of Liberty - United States Holocaust Memorial Museum, courtesy of Anita Willens

Back cover of *Deutschland* - https://en.wikipedia.org/wiki/SS_Deutschland_(1900)

## ACKNOWLEDGEMENTS

I wish to express my appreciation to the Oprah Winfrey Network (OWN) for capturing the reunion of Edith and Gerda on film and licensing the screen captures for use in this book. I am grateful to the Ragdale Foundation for a writer's residency during which time I completed the manuscript. It has been a privilege to work with Tom Greensfelder, whose exceptional vision in designing *Like Finding My Twin* is evident on every page. Finally, this book would not have been possible without the generous spirit of my mother, Edith Westerfeld Schumer, whose life continues to inspire me.

*Author Fern Schumer Chapman (right), and her mother,*
*Edith Westerfeld Schumer (left).*

...s expierenced really...
...nged my life. I...
...so ha...

...dith,
...ent through so much...
a very strong Person.
...nk you for being
...ling to come to our
lotsof Respect
Jon Sobieski

...log with us
and allowing us to
find your dear old
friend.

sincerly
Mark

I really think th...
Gerda was very...
felt like I was a...
something to the pa...

...to Madison. Whe...
heared about you...
Gera I felt so sad...
seperated from so...
your so close to is...
terrible, I'm so g...
You two have bee...
reunited.
-H

I wanted to see
you and Gerda reunited
because it would
give us all a chance
to repair some of
the near-illega...
damage cause...
Nazis...

your story has taught...
me what to really
apprecicite in life.
your story was
so inspiring that
it broke my heart
to have to see you two
leave eachother. I am
so glad I could help
and am so excited that
you two will meet
again!
~Bridget R...

...hank you...
for sharing...
amazing sto...
with us! I ho...
always wan...
to help bu...
couldn't a...
...time...

Edith,
This has to be short but I
just wanted to know how
thankful I am that we found
Gerda. I honestly cannot even
imagine how hard it must
have been to lose a best
friend AND be sent to the
U.S. (an unknown place for you
at the time) ...have...
a great...
and it's...
you are...

When I heard your story, I didn't
know that we were going to
help. After we had learned we
had found Edith, I felt good
to be apart of it. I'm glad
two old friends could recom...
...t. I couldn't imagine
...ing 73 years with o...
...king one of mine.

When I heard your story and
wanting to find Gertie, I was so
moved. My classmates, teacher and
I wanted to help so bad. This whole
process has been so inspiring.
We were so obsessed with trying
to reunite you and Gertie!
Your story means so much.
My grandma's friends actually were
in concentration camps! I hope you
have a great time in seattle!
~Jennifer Wadning

When I heard your story
I found it very sad that
Edith could not find the
one person she could relate
with and so it makes me
happy that I could help with
finding...

When I fist heard the stor...
I felt...
I wanted t...so something...
When Mrs. O'Boyle told us...
we would look for her I was...

...this stor...
...you? Di...
...back or...
...mories...
...it was...
...back togeth...
...you

...was very t...
...id you a...
...up it m...
...t to d...
...hat we...
...you w...
...again